Presented to

Dear Precious Hours

By RAMONA M.

On the Occasion of

CHRISTMAS

Date 2009

© 2009 by Barbour Publishing, Inc.

Compiled by Kathy Shutt.

ISBN 978-1-60260-613-5

Several text selections were compiled from the following: *365 Secrets to a Happy Life, 365 Days of Praise, 365 Meditations for the Satisfied Soul,* and *365 Days to Jump-Start Your Prayer Life,* published by Barbour Publishing, Inc.

Text on days 6–9, 15, 20–22, 27–29, 43–44, 57, 59, 62–68, 97–100, 123, 130, 137–138, 142–147, 162–166, 168–170, 176–181, 187, 189, 191–193, 201–203, 206, 221–222, 224–225, 233–234, 240–241, 260, 262–265, 268–269, 293, 315–316, 318, 321–326, 328, 330, 332, 338–339, 343–348, 353–356, 358, 361, 363 by Pamela McQuade.
Text on days 13, 19, 31, 52–55, 104–105, 107–110, 112–120, 125, 131, 207–208, 210, 214, 239, 242, 250, 252, 311 by Hannah Whitall Smith.

Published by Barbour Publishing, Inc., P.O. Box 719, Uhrichsville, Ohio 44683, www.barbourbooks.com

Our mission is to publish and distribute inspirational products offering exceptional value and biblical encouragement to the masses.

Member of the
Evangelical Christian
Publishers Association

Printed in India.

WHISPERS OF
Promise

BARBOUR
PUBLISHING

Praise God

Let my teaching fall like rain
and my words descend like dew,
like showers on new grass, like
abundant rain on tender plants.
I will proclaim the name of the
LORD. Oh, praise the greatness
of our God! He is the Rock, his
works are perfect, and all his ways
are just. A faithful God who does
no wrong, upright and just is he.

DEUTERONOMY 32:2–4 NIV

From Within

All [God's] glory and beauty come from within, and there He delights to dwell. His visits there are frequent, His conversations sweet, His comforts refreshing, His peace passing all understanding.

THOMAS À KEMPIS

Everything New

Everything that is new or uncommon raises a pleasure in the imagination because it fills the soul with an agreeable surprise, gratifies its curiosity, and gives it an idea of which it was not before possessed.

JOSEPH ADDISON

Youth Is. . .

Youth is not a time of life; it is a state of mind; it is not a matter of rosy cheeks, red lips, and supple knees; it is a matter of the will, quality of the imagination, a vigor of the emotions; it is the freshness of the deep springs of the soul.

SAMUEL ULLMAN

From Grace to Grace

From faith to faith,
   from grace to grace,
So in Thy strength shall I go on,
Till heaven and earth
   flee from Thy face,
And glory end what grace begun.

WOLFGANG DESSLER

Mission Accomplished

One day, we won't have to settle
for brief spells of soul satisfaction.
We'll spend all eternity singing
God praises for the victories He
gave us on earth. Our mission
accomplished, we'll fill heaven with
the rejoicing of satisfied souls.

Sin's Proper Place

We might like to think Christianity
has more hours of sitting on
our laurels than of battle. None
of us prefers hard work to the
blessings of peace, yet we can't
have one without the other. God's
sanctification is worked out in
our lives with effort, and no one
achieves spiritual growth only by
singing psalms. That restful part
of our lives blesses us between the
battles that put sin in its proper
place behind us.

Soul Satisfaction

Everyone looks for satisfaction
in many ways and in many areas
of their lives. We all want to feel
fulfilled. But the person who
experiences satisfaction on the
job, in a marriage, and in other
areas can remain empty if the
soul is ignored. Christians have
learned that soul satisfaction is an
unsurpassed delight, and it comes
only from one place: Jesus.

All He Has, All He Is

As we look at God's greatness
and experience His love, awe fills
our beings. Our scant ability to
appreciate His personality and
power lay bare our own smallness.
Yet when the Creator points out our
frailties, He's not belittling us. He
reminds us that He wants to share
all He has and all He is with us.

This New Day

This bright, new day complete
with twenty-four hours of
opportunities, choices, and
attitudes comes with a perfectly
matched set of 1,440 minutes.
This unique gift, this one day,
cannot be exchanged, replaced, or
refunded. Handle with care. Make
the most of it.

Element of Joy

Into our lives, in many simple,
familiar, homely ways, God
infuses this element of joy
from the surprises of life,
which unexpectedly brighten our
days, and fill our eyes with light.

HENRY WADSWORTH LONGFELLOW

Life

Life is what we are alive to.
It is not length but breadth. . . .
Be alive to. . .goodness, purity,
love, history, poetry, music,
flowers, stars, God, and eternal
hope.

MALTBIE D. BABCOCK

Trust

A great many people do everything
but trust. As if to attempt to fly
with one wing, they try vigorously
and wonder why it is that they do
not mount up, never dreaming
that it is because all the while the
wing of trust is hanging idle by
their sides.

Unlimited Love

Everything which relates to God
is infinite. We must therefore,
while we keep our hearts humble,
keep our aims high. Our highest
services are indeed but finite,
imperfect. But as God is unlimited
in goodness, He should have our
unlimited love.

HANNAH MORE

Freedom

Caught up in their own independence, unbelievers have missed out on the truth that they aren't really free at all: They can't seem to do good. They'll never know otherwise unless they see someone who is free indeed. Who knows what simple act could help another understand your freedom to do right, not just to do what you want?

Promise of a Better Day

From far beyond our world of
trouble and care and change, our
Lord shines with undimmed light,
a radiant, guiding Star to all who
will follow Him. . . .

CHARLES E. HURLBURT AND T. C. HORTON

An Irish Blessing

May the road rise up to meet you,
may the wind always be at your
back, the sun shine warm upon
your face. . .and until we meet
again, may God hold you in the
palm of His hand.

Love Works Miracles

Love is the divine vitality that
everywhere produces and restores
life. To each and every one of
us, it gives the power of working
miracles if we will.

LYDIA MARIA CHILD

Security

When we are told that God,
who is our dwelling place, is also
our fortress, it can mean one
thing, and that is, that if we will
but live in our dwelling place, we
shall be perfectly safe and secure.

Unexpected Joys

Without God's help I could never
have completed an extraordinarily
difficult task He honored me with.
Alone, the work He ordained
would have turned into a thankless
chore. But the eternally faithful
One combined the task with
so many unexpected joys that
thankfulness never became
a problem. Despite a host of
troubles, I received all I needed.

Witnessing

Faith, lived out consistently,
may turn some doubting hearts to
the Savior. Then instead of being
horrified by their wrong judgment,
they too, will share the blessing
when every knee bows to Jesus.
We who once deserved
condemnation have seen it turned
aside for mercy. Let's share that
with as many as we can.

You'll Never Stand Alone

God doesn't want to see you suffer
unnecessarily. Instead of leaving
you to work out your life in your
own way, He wants to guide you.
When you face difficult days. . .you
won't stand alone. Trouble won't
blast your life but will strengthen
you instead. Your Creator can turn
all trials to blessings if you just
stand firm in Him. Enjoy your
days in Jesus.

Power in Prayer

When I learn to pray not only
for my immediate interests but
enlarge my heart to take in the
whole church and the whole world,
my supplication will have power
with God.

Andrew Murray

Children Are a Gift

God sends children. . .to enlarge
our hearts, to make us unselfish,
and full of kindly sympathies and
affections; to give our souls higher
aims, to call out all our faculties to
extended enterprise and exertion;
to bring round our fireside bright
faces and happy smiles, and loving,
tender hearts.

MARY HOWITT

Rivers of Living Waters

You never can measure what God will do through you. . . . Keep your relationship right with Him, then whatever circumstances you are in, and whoever you meet day by day, He is pouring rivers of living water through you.

OSWALD CHAMBERS

We Must Sail

I find the great thing in this world
is not so much where we stand,
as in what direction we are
moving. To reach the port of
heaven, we must sail sometimes
with the wind and sometimes
against it, but we must sail, and
not drift, nor lie at anchor.

OLIVER WENDELL HOLMES

All Things Work Together for Good

Nothing that happens is beyond the Lord's domain. Nothing can touch us that the heavenly Father can't deal with, and no event can ruin His plan for good in our lives. All things, He promises, will work together for our good, if we love Him (Romans 8:28).

Let's Lighten the Darkness

When we reach out in faith to
someone and don't get a positive
response, do we recognize that
we're speaking to a spiritually deaf
soul? . . . Kindness in the face of
opposition may begin the work
that opens deaf ears and lightens
blind eyes. Let's start to unclog
ears and lighten the darkness.

Each Day

If only we could trust God
perfectly each day and rise
constantly up, higher on the
mountains. . . . We'd like to
think that's an ideal Christian
experience. But our spiritual
landscape does not consist
simply of mountains. Valleys lie
between the uplands. And without
the valleys, there would be no
mountains at all.

Be Transformed

Do not conform any longer to the pattern of this world, but be transformed by the renewing of your mind. Then you will be able to test and approve what God's will is—his good, pleasing and perfect will.

ROMANS 12:2 NIV

Sanctification

Sanctification is both a step of
faith and a process of works.
It is a step of surrender and trust
on our part, and it is a process of
development on God's part.

The Love of Christ

That Christ may dwell in your
hearts by faith; that ye, being
rooted and grounded in love,
may be able to comprehend will
all saints what is the breadth, and
length, and depth, and height;
and to know the love of Christ,
which passeth knowledge, that ye
might be filled with all the fulness
of God.

EPHESIANS 3:17–19 KJV

A Secure Home

The Bible does not say very much
about homes; it says a great deal
about the things that make them.
It speaks about life and love and
joy and peace and rest. If we get a
house and put these into it,
we shall have a secured home.

JOHN HENRY JOWETT

Walk without Fear

We walk without fear, full of hope and courage and strength to do His will, waiting for the endless good which He is always giving as fast as He can get us able to take it in.

GEORGE MACDONALD

Abundant Grace

The Lord's chief desire is to reveal
Himself to you and, in order for
Him to do that, He gives you
abundant grace. The Lord gives
you the experience of enjoying His
presence. He touches you, and His
touch is so delightful that,
more than ever, you are drawn
inwardly to Him.

MADAME JEANNE GUYON

Answer to Prayer

When I know what it is to abide
in Christ and to yield to the Holy
Spirit, I begin to learn that God
will give power in answer to prayer.

ANDREW MURRAY

Happiness Is a Sunbeam

Happiness is a sunbeam. . . . When
it strikes a kindred heart, like the
converged lights upon a mirror,
it reflects with redoubled
brightness. It is not perfected until
it is shared.

JANE PORTER

An Unfinished Symphony

This life is not all. It is an "unfinished symphony". . .with him who knows that he is related to God and has felt "the power of an endless life."

HENRY WARD BEECHER

Amazing Grace!

Amazing grace!
How sweet the sound
That saved a wretch like me!
I once was lost, but now am found;
Was blind, but now I see.

JOHN NEWTON

Look to the Bow

Trust God where you cannot trace
Him. Do not try to penetrate the
cloud He brings over you;
rather look to the bow that is on it.
The mystery is God's; the promise
is yours.

JOHN R. MACDUFF

A New Day

Finish every day and be done
with it. You have done what you
could. . . . Tomorrow is a new day;
begin it well and serenely and with
too high a spirit to be cumbered
with your old nonsense. This
day is all that is good and fair.
It is too dear, with its hopes and
invitations, to waste a moment on
yesterday.

RALPH WALDO EMERSON

Completely Loved

We are so preciously loved by God
that we cannot even comprehend
it. No created being can ever know
how much and how sweetly and
tenderly God loves them.

Joyful Prayer

Has prayer become mechanical,
a chore instead of a joy?
Remember how beloved you are
by the One you're speaking to. He
doesn't want to hear the details
of just anyone's life—He's asked
you to share with Him, and you're
blessed to know His love.

Our Father

Like a father, God never gives up
on us, even in our disobedience.
But just because He forgives, we
can't take advantage by forgetting
He is still Lord of the universe or
by treating Him without respect.
Because He loves us, He doesn't
hold the sin against us, but our
Lord disciplines unrepentant
children. If He didn't do that,
He wouldn't be our Father.

The Mark God Sets

Beauty is the mark God sets on
virtue. Every natural action is
graceful; every heroic act is also
decent, and causes the place and
the bystanders to shine.

RALPH WALDO EMERSON

I Will Praise You

Send forth your light and your
truth, let them guide me; let them
bring me to your holy mountain,
to the place where you dwell.
Then will I go to the altar of God,
to God, my joy and delight. I will
praise you with the harp, O God,
my God.

PSALM 43:3–4 NIV

Virtue

Let grace and goodness be
the principal loadstone of thy
affections. For love, which hath
ends, will have an end; whereas
that which is founded on true
virtue will always continue.

JOHN DRYDEN

My Anchor Holds

And it holds, my anchor holds;
Blow your wildest then, O gale,
On my bark so small and frail,
By His grace I shall not fail,
For my anchor holds,
My anchor holds.

W. C. MARTIN

Grace

Grace, when it comes to us,
is like a firebrand dropped into
the sea, where it would certainly
be quenched were it not of such a
miraculous quality that it baffles
the water—floods, and sets up its
reign of fire and light even in the
depths.

CHARLES H. SPURGEON

Unexpected Success

If one advances confidently in
the direction of his dreams,
and endeavors to live the life
which he has imagined, he will
meet with a success unexpected in
common hours. Go confidently in
the direction of your dreams! Live
the life you imagined.

HENRY DAVID THOREAU

Imagination

The imagination is the spur of
delights. . .all depend upon it,
it is the mainspring of everything;
now, is it not by means of the
imagination one knows joy? Is it
not of the imagination that the
sharpest pleasures arise?

MARQUIS DE SADE

Wholly into His Hands

A positive transformation is to take place. We have most of us tried to do it for ourselves and have grievously failed. The Lord Jesus has come on purpose to do it for all who put themselves wholly into His hands.

Grow Up into Christ

The maturity of Christian
experience cannot be reached in
a moment but is the result of the
work of God's Holy Spirit who,
by His energizing and
transforming power, causes us to
grow up into Christ in all things.

Thankful for Trials

Let us be thankful for every
trial that will help to destroy our
earthly chariots and that will
compel us to take refuge in the
chariot of God, which stands ready
and waiting beside us in every
event and circumstance of life.

Careful for Nothing

Let the ways of childish confidence
and freedom from care. . .teach
you what should be your ways with
God. Leaving yourselves in His
hands, learn to be literally "careful
for nothing."

Widening Ripples

Do a deed of simple kindness;
Though its end you may not see,
It may reach, like widening ripples,
Down a long eternity.

JOSEPH PARKER NORRIS

Roar with Joy!

Like the earth, we Christians
rejoice at the idea that Jesus will
come. Though we've already begun
to experience God's changes in
our souls, one day everything
about us will be made new in Him.
Everything will be spanking clean,
ready to worship the Creator.
That's something to roar with joy
about!

Open Doors

Open your mouth and taste, open
your eyes and see—how good GOD
is. Blessed are you who run to him.
Worship GOD if you want the best;
worship opens doors to all his
goodness.

PSALM 34:8–9 MSG

Priceless

We may not reach around the
world to people. But that doesn't
mean God doesn't value all we do.
Though each believer may only
touch a few lives, that impact may
go far beyond what can be seen.
In the end, God may show the
whole world that the blessed
silver-tongued saint who lived
down the street was priceless to
Him and His work.

Never Lose an Opportunity

Never lose an opportunity
of seeing anything that is
beautiful; for beauty is God's
handwriting—a wayside
sacrament. Welcome it in every
fair face, in every fair sky, in every
fair flower, and thank God for it as
a cup of blessing.

RALPH WALDO EMERSON

In Secret

"But when you pray, go into your
room, close the door and pray to
your Father, who is unseen.
Then your Father, who sees what is
done in secret, will reward you."

MATTHEW 6:6 NIV

God's Child

You are God's child. That might
seem a rather ordinary thing,
but consider it more carefully,
and feel the amazement of that
truth. The Creator of the universe,
the all-powerful God, wants to be
your daddy (after all, that's what
abba means). This awesome Being
wants you to trust Him and seek
His love and protection.

Sweet Release

When we place a trouble in God's
hands then take His advice,
seemingly unsolvable problems
slip away or are lightened by our
sharing them with the Savior.
It's not magic, but a sweet release.
Working hard on our own,
we create only stress, worry, and
more uncertainty. Only resting in
Him brings the answer to every
need.

Learning Brings Delight!

The water of salvation doesn't come from a fountain, but a well. It won't automatically flow into our lives, whether or not we desire it. Christian growth doesn't happen without our will. We must draw it up in our lives, making the effort to bring it from the deep places. The effort of coming to Him and learning more of His nature brings delight.

Faith Never Changes

Whether we're bounding along in faith, or struggling through a doleful valley, our faith does not change. We still trust in the One who made both the mountains and valleys, and He'll faithfully see us through either.

Guidelines

Truly successful relationships are based on God. Those who know the Word, follow God faithfully, and live what He has taught them won't have perfect relationships, but they can develop increasingly better ones as they follow the guidelines of the Master.

A "God-Shaped Hole"

No one can destroy the joy that
wells up from knowing Jesus.
People who don't know Him don't
have a well. Their lives are dry
and empty. They may be good at
covering up that fact with a smile
or jokes, but deep inside is what
St. Augustine described as a
"God-shaped hole."

Heart Change

Heart change may not happen
overnight, but with faith and
determination to follow God's
Word, we'll see amazing changes.
As God's healing water seeps
into our lives, the trickle touches
our souls and change becomes
possible. And as we open ourselves
to His will and way, the trickle
springs up, becomes a stream,
a pool, then a river of love. And all
of it started in God's hand.

He Never Sleeps

What God's almighty power hath
made His gracious mercy keepeth,
By morning glow or evening shade
His watchful eye ne'er sleepeth.
Within the kingdom of His might,
Lo! All is just and all is right:
To God all praise and glory!

JOHANN J. SCHUTZ

God's Promises

We may. . .depend upon God's
promises, for. . .He will be as good
as His word. He is so kind that He
cannot deceive us, so true that He
cannot break His promises.

MATTHEW HENRY

The Real Gift

This is the real gift: We have been given the breath of life, designed with a unique, one-of-a-kind soul that lives forever—whether we live our life as a joy or with indifference doesn't change the fact that we've been given the gift of being now and forever. Priceless in value, we are handcrafted by God, who has a personal design and plan for each of us.

Make Me a Channel

Lord, make me a channel of Your
peace. Where there is hatred,
let me bring love. Where there is
offense, forgiveness. Where there
is discord, reconciliation. Where
there is doubt, faith. Where there
is despair, hope. Where there
is sadness, joy. Where there is
darkness, Your light.

ST. FRANCIS OF ASSISI

Real, Permanent Joy

Real joy and peace do not depend
on power, kingly wealth, or other
material possessions. . . . This real
and permanent joy is found only
in the kingdom of God, which is
established in the heart when we
are born again.

SADHU SUNDAR SINGH

Humble Instruments

God does not so much want us to
do things as to let people see what
He can do. God is not looking
for extraordinary characters
as His instruments, but He is
looking for humble instruments
through whom He can be honored
throughout the ages.

A. B. SIMPSON

Learn to Be Content

I have learned to be content
whatever the circumstances. I
know what it is to be in need,
and I know what it is to have
plenty. I have learned the secret
of being content in any and every
situation, whether well fed or
hungry, whether living in plenty or
in want.

PHILIPPIANS 4:11–12 NIV

I Long For. . .

I long for scenes where man has
   never trod;
A place where woman has never
   smil'd or wept;
There to abide with my creator,
   God,
And sleep as I in childhood
   sweetly slept;
Untroubling and untroubled
   where I lie;
The grass below—above the
   vaulted sky.

JOHN CLARE

Grace Abounds

No one was ever saved because his sins were small; no one was ever rejected on account of the greatness of his sins. Where sin abounded, grace shall much more abound.

ARCHIBALD ALEXANDER

Always Available

Grace is available for each of
us every day. . .but we've got to
remember to ask for it with a
grateful heart and not worry about
whether there will be enough for
tomorrow.

SARAH BAN BREATHNACH

Cherish. . .

Cherish your visions; cherish your
ideals; cherish the music that
stirs in your heart, the beauty that
forms in your mind, the loveliness
that drapes your purest thoughts,
for out of them will grow all
delightful conditions, all heavenly
environment.

JAMES ALLEN

Grace Is Free

Grace is free, but when once you
take it you are bound forever to
the giver, and bound to catch the
spirit of the giver. Like produces
like, grace makes you gracious,
the giver makes you give.

E. STANLEY JONES

Do Good to All

Do all the good you can, by all the
means you can, in all the ways you
can, in all the places you can, at all
the times you can, as long as ever
you can.

JOHN WESLEY

Teach Me. . .

Teach me, O Lord, to do your
will; teach me to live worthily and
humbly in Your sight; for You are
my Wisdom, who know me truly,
and who knew me before the world
was made, and before I had my
being.

THOMAS À KEMPIS

The Way

He is the Way. . .the only Way
which leads directly to the
Father. . . . When we walk in
the Way, we walk in the light.
We journey with Himself in sweet
fellowship. What a joyful journey!
The Way is lightened by His
countenance. He holds us by the
hand. He supplies our needs.
What a Savior!

CHARLES E. HURLBURT AND T. C. HORTON

Timeless

In such a beautiful wilderness of
wildflowers we are amused with
the very variety and novelty of
the scene so much that we in our
pleasure lose all sense of weariness
and fatigue in the length of our
wanderings and get to the end
before we are aware of our journey.

JOHN CLARE

The Light of Life

I heard the voice of Jesus say:
"I am this dark world's light; look
unto Me, thy morn shall rise,
and all thy day be bright." I looked
to Jesus, and I found in Him my
Star, my Sun; and in that light of
life, I'll walk till traveling days are
done!

HORATIUS BONAR

Loving God

We are of such value to God that
He came to live among us. . .and
to guide us home. He will go to
any length to seek us, even to
being lifted high upon the cross to
draw us back to Himself. We can
only respond by loving God for
His love.

CATHERINE OF SIENA

Two Requirements

There are two requirements for our proper enjoyment of earthly blessing which God bestows on us—a thankful reflection on the goodness of the Giver, and a deep sense of the unworthiness of the receiver. The first would make us grateful, the second humble.

HANNAH MORE

Love the Lord with All of Your Heart

How sympathetically loving is our Lord with our unbelief. How patient He is, yet how He longs for our unquestioning, implicit faith. Let us honor Him by believing Him with all our heart.

CHARLES E. HURLBURT AND T. C. HORTON

Lift Up Our Thoughts, Lord

O Lord God, in whom we live,
and move, and have our being,
open our eyes that we may behold
Thy Fatherly presence ever about
us. Draw our hearts to Thee with
the power of Thy love. . . . Lift our
thoughts up to Thee in heaven,
and make us to know that all
things are possible to us through
Thy Son, our Redeemer.

BROOKE FOSS WESTCOTT

Forever

Give thanks to the LORD, for he
is good. His love endures forever.
Give thanks to the God of gods.
His love endures forever. Give
thanks to the Lord of lords: His
love endures forever. To him who
alone does great wonders, his love
endures forever.

PSALM 136:1–4 NIV

Your Redeemer's Strength

Trust in your Redeemer's strength. . . . Exercise what faith you have, and by and by, He shall rise upon you with healing beneath His wings. Go from faith to faith, and you shall receive blessing upon blessing.

CHARLES H. SPURGEON

Satisfied

I have seen you in the sanctuary
and beheld your power and your
glory. Because your love is better
than life, my lips will glorify you.
I will praise you as long as I live,
and in your name I will lift up my
hands. My soul will be satisfied as
with the richest of foods;
with singing lips my mouth
will praise you.

PSALM 63:2–5 NIV

Count Your Blessings

Count your blessings;
  name them one by one.
Count your blessings;
  see what God has done!
Count your blessings;
  name them one by one.
Count your many blessings;
  see what God has done!

JOHNSON OATMAN JR.

Our Father's Business

God is a kind Father. He sets us all
in the places where He wishes us to
be employed; and that employment
is truly "our Father's business."
He chooses work for every creature
that will be delightful to them if
they do it simply and humbly.

Without Him Nothing, With Him All Things!

What a foundation for our faith when we know that Jesus was the Word and the Word was God. . . . As we feel the throb of our heart, there is a voice that says, "God!" As we look upon the heavens and the clouds—"God!" The sun, the moon, the trees, the flowers, the living creatures, all are saying, "God!" Without Him—nothing! With Him—all things!

I Love You

My love of You, O Lord, is not some vague feeling: it is positive and certain. Your Word struck into my heart and from that moment I loved You. Besides this, all about me, heaven and earth and all that they contain proclaim that I should love You.

ST. AUGUSTINE

A Solution for Every Burden

Is there a burden you bear that
God isn't interested in? Whatever
you face day by day, if you haven't
brought it before Jesus,
you're carrying an unnecessary
load. You see, God doesn't expect
of us more than we can manage.
God has a solution for every
burden- bearer. He offers to
shoulder our hardships—all of
them—for us.

Springs of Faith

What's true of creation is true
of us: We, too, are incredibly
complex. Our hearts may hurt for
years over a series of wrongs;
as they work deep into our souls,
they work on our spirits and
thoughts in convoluted ways. But
just as God perfectly understands
our world, He sees into our hurt
hearts and spirits. And He can
alter a river of hate or doubt into
springs of faith and trust.

The Path before Us

God doesn't promise a piece-of-cake lifestyle. He won't so smooth our roads that we never bounce around, but He will see that while we're driving them, we don't break an axle. With His power, we can keep on traveling the path He's set before us.

God Rules Our Lives

Dry to wet or wet to dry, God
changes the world at His will,
ruling over it in ways we often
don't understand. But deserts and
rivers aren't the only things God
rules. Though we may question
or rebel against this truth,
God also rules our lives.

A Means of Grace

Difficulty in prayer is a means
of grace. If I only had to kneel,
ask, get, and go away, loss to my
spiritual life would result.

ANDREW MURRAY

Surrender

In the quietness of prayer let
me believe that a simple and
determined surrender of my will to
Him will bring the heartcleansing
I need.

ANDREW MURRAY

Give Your Life to God

What a change it would make if
secret prayer were not only asking
for knowledge or strength,
but the giving of my life into the
safekeeping of a faithful God.

God Is the Giver

From beginning to end, God is
the giver and we are the receivers;
and it is not to those who do great
things but to those who receive
abundance of grace and the gift
of righteousness that the richest
promises are made.

Ask and Receive

This blessed life must not be
looked upon as an attainment but
as an obtainment. We cannot earn
it; we cannot climb up to it;
we cannot win it; we can do nothing
but ask for it and receive it.

Do Not Fear

Do not fear, for I am with you;
do not be dismayed, for I am your
God. I will strengthen you and
help you; I will uphold you with my
righteous right hand.

ISAIAH 41:10 NIV

Let Christ Live in Us

We must put off our self-life by
faith continually and put on the
life of Christ; and we must do this,
not only by faith, but practically as
well. We must continually put self
to death in all the details of daily
life and must let God instead live
and work in us.

Happiest and Most Restful

We must give up all liberty
of choice. We mean a life of
inevitable obedience. To a soul
ignorant of God, this may look
hard; but to those who know Him,
it is the happiest and most restful
of lives.

God Delivers Us

Abandon yourselves so utterly to
the Lord Jesus Christ that He may
be able to, by the law of the Spirit
of life in Himself, deliver you
from every other law that could
possibly enslave you.

Just Believe

The whole secret of the Christian
life that I have been trying to
describe is revealed in the child
relationship. Nothing more is
needed than to believe that God
is as good a Father as the ideal
earthly father.

Dews of Quietness

Drop Thy still dews of quietness,
Till all our strivings cease;
Take from our souls
    the strain and stress,
And let our ordered lives confess
The beauty of Thy peace.

John G. Whittier

Infinity

Put together all the tenderest love
you know of, the deepest you have
ever felt and the strongest that
has ever been poured out upon
you, and heap upon it all the love
of all the loving human hearts in
the world, and then multiply it by
infinity, and you will begin perhaps
to have some faint glimpses of the
love and grace of God!

Divine Love

Divine love is tender and self-sacrificing and devoted, glad to bear and forbear and suffer, and eager to lavish its best gifts and blessings upon the objects of its love.

New Creatures

God is a great deal more concerned about our really being new creatures than about anything else, because He knows that if we are right as to our inward being, we shall certainly do right as to our outward actions.

Bask in the Sunshine

Bask in the sunshine of His love. Drink of the living waters of His goodness. Keep your face upturned to Him as the flowers do to the sun. Look, and your soul shall live and grow.

Inward Refreshment

Since, therefore, God is sure to
have His own way concerning
those who abandon themselves to
Him in perfect trust, into what
wonderful green pastures of inward
rest and beside what blessedly still
waters of inward refreshment will
He lead all such!

Let God Work

We must lay down all the activity
of the creature as such and must
let only the activities of God work
in us and through us and by us.
Self must step aside to let God
work.

Untouchable

No man or company of men,
no power in earth or heaven
can touch that soul which is
abiding in Christ without first
passing through His encircling
presence and receiving the seal
of permission.

All Must Be Accepted

Surely He is a husbandman we
can trust; and if He sends storms,
or winds, or rains, or sunshine,
all must be accepted at His
hands with the most unwavering
confidence that He will bring us to
maturity who knows the very best
way of accomplishing His end.

Abiding Peace

As the violet abides peacefully
in its little place, content to
receive its daily portion without
concerning itself about the
wandering of the winds or the
falling of the rain, so we must
repose in the present moment as it
comes to us from God.

Show Me Your Ways

Show me your ways, O Lord,
teach me your paths; guide me in
your truth and teach me, for you
are God my Savior, and my hope is
in you all day long. Remember,
O Lord, your great mercy and
love, for they are from of old.

PSALM 25:4–6 NIV

How Much You Mean to Him

I am God, your personal God,
The Holy of Israel, your Savior.
I paid a huge price for you. . . .
That's how much you mean to me!
That's how much I love you! I'd
sell off the whole world to get you
back, trade the creation just for
you. So don't be afraid:
I'm with you.

ISAIAH 43:3–5 MSG

God Bears Our Burdens

God will bear our burdens, but
if we don't want to give them to
Him, He will let us struggle along
on our own for a while. He won't
insist we do things His way but will
let us learn how heavy the burdens
really are. When our backs are
tired and we can't take another
step, He'll remind us that He was
always willing to carry them for
us. Is He reminding you of that
today?

Created for Him

When we are born again, we are brought into the realization of God's great purpose for the human race, namely, that He created us for Himself. This realization of our election by God is the most joyful on earth, and we must learn to rely on this tremendous creative purpose of God.

OSWALD CHAMBERS

Know My Heart. . .

In order to prevent failure or to
discover its cause, if we find we
have failed, it is necessary to keep
continually before us this prayer:
"Search me, O God, and know my
heart."

The Spirit's Prayer

God. . .with a loving Father's
heart, is always searching our
hearts to find the Spirit's prayer
and to answer it. . . . And when we
reach our heavenly home and read
the records of life, we shall better
know and appreciate the infinite
love of that Divine Friend who
has watched within as the Spirit of
prayer and breathed out our every
need to the heart of God.

Some Day!

Some day when fades
   the golden sun
Beneath the rosy tinted west,
My blessed Lord will say,
   "Well done!"
And I shall enter into rest.

FANNY CROSBY

"Man of Sorrows"

He who was the source of all joy,
the giver of all peace, He before
whom angels and archangels bow
in adoration, is also called a "Man
of Sorrows." Grief broke His
heart, crushed out His life. . . .
He sorrowed all alone. . . . But He
shares thy grief; He carries all thy
sorrow and comforts those who
trust Him. Shall we not worship
and adore the Man of Sorrows?

CHARLES E. HURLBURT AND T. C. HORTON

Richly Blessed

I asked for strength that I might
achieve; I was made weak that
I might learn humbly to obey.
I asked for health that I might
do greater things; I was given
infirmity that I might do better
things. . . . I got nothing that I
asked for, but everything that I
had hoped for. Almost despite
myself, my unspoken prayers were
answered; I am, among all men,
most richly blessed.

UNKNOWN CONFEDERATE SOLDIER

In His Time

Will God rescue us from trouble?
When we ask and He doesn't seem
to answer, the pressure cooker
we're in may steam up our faith,
too. Like David, we may question
if God will come to our aid before
we're cooked (Psalm 35:17–18).
When you need help, bring every
concern before your Lord.
Then trust God and thank Him
that He will come through for
you—in His time.

Superior Care

The truth really is that His care is infinitely superior to any possibilities of human care and that He, who counts the very hairs of our heads, takes note of the minutest matters that affect the lives of His children.

We Are Not Our Own

We are not our own, any more
than what we possess is our own.
We did not make ourselves;
we cannot be supreme over
ourselves. We cannot be our own
masters. We are God's property
by creation, by redemption, by
regeneration.

JOHN HENRY NEWMAN

Passover

The day of resurrection,
  earth tell it out abroad!
The Passover of gladness,
  the Passover of God.
From death to life eternal,
  from this world to the sky,
Our Christ has brought us over,
  with hymns of victory.

JOHN OF DAMASCUS

Calm Me, O Lord

Calm me, O Lord,
   as You stilled the storm,
Still me, O Lord;
   keep me from harm.
Let all the tumult within me cease,
Enfold me, Lord, in your peace.

CELTIC TRADITIONAL

Wounded for Me

Our Savior pictures Himself not merely as the Rock of Ages, and our Strong Rock of Refuge, but the Rock of our Salvation. . . . In Him and upon His merit and atoning grace, we were saved from among the lost. Let us glory in this precious name and never forget that He was "wounded for our transgressions" and "that he bore our sins in his own body on the tree."

CHARLES E. HURLBURT AND T. C. HORTON

Nothing Is Impossible

"Assuredly, I say to you, if you have
faith as a mustard seed, you will
say to this mountain, 'Move from
here to there,' and it will move;
and nothing will be impossible for
you."

MATTHEW 17:20 NKJV

Our Hope Is in God

All our hopes lie in the One who provides rivers of truth to water our thirsty souls. When we've drunk deeply, His river overflows our lives and splashes into the hearts and minds of those we live and work with. Their thirst quenched, they convey it on to others, and the river of faith swells again.

Delight in His Presence

"Count your blessings" is a popular
phrase I've never related to very
well. The moment I try to list all
God has done for me, I realize
I can hardly cover everything
adequately. So instead of detailing
every benefit God provides,
I'll thank Him for a few big ones
and spend time basking in His
love. As I look closely into my
Lord's face, I can't help but delight
in His presence.

What Next?

You do not know what you are
going to do; the only thing you
know is that God knows what He
is doing. . . . It is this attitude that
keeps you in perpetual wonder—
you do not know what God is
going to do next.

OSWALD CHAMBERS

Beauty and Wonder of the World

I still find each day too short for
all the thoughts I want to think,
all the walks I want to take, all the
books I want to read, and all the
friends I want to see. The longer
I live, the more my mind dwells
upon the beauty and wonder of the
world.

JOHN BURROUGHS

The Fragrance

But thanks be to God, who always leads us in triumphal procession in Christ and through us spreads everywhere the fragrance of the knowledge of him. For we are to God the aroma of Christ among those who are being saved and those who are perishing.

2 CORINTHIANS 2:14–15 NIV

Knowing God

Nothing in this world is better
than knowing God. Eternal
delights cannot compare to
anything here on earth—even
the best of the blessings God's
already given us. Our hearts are
no longer earthbound, and we long
to be with Him. Though we may
not rush to leave the fellowship
of friends and family, the beauty
of this world, and so much more
that God has given, we appreciate
that life here, without God's love,
would be meaningless.

Worth Standing

In a day when dishonesty is often almost taken as a matter of course, a person whose strength of character demands honesty can stand out in a crowd. Sometimes it's the kind of standing out. . .that leads to uncomfortable situations. But there are things worth standing for, even if they have a price. Sometimes that price is just what brings the blessing.

Rooted in Jesus

Christians can have several kinds of root systems. Some are shallow, so when a storm comes along, they're easily uprooted. Then there are those who send down a deep taproot, like a maple tree, which grips the earth with an impressive power. God meant every believer to grow strong in Him. We can never be too rooted in Jesus.

Awed

As we get to know Jesus more
closely—as we peer into His face
and understand more completely
just who He is—we are awed by
His strength and humbled by His
desire to share even that with us.
The more we seek Him, the more
His strength can empower all of
our life.

Powerful Blessing

Do you feel as if you can't go on?
Jesus can keep you going by His
power, and as His Spirit fills you,
you'll know that even if you're
fighting tooth and nail,
you'll eventually win in Him.
God's might is not something He
uses to make us see things His way
or to take control over us. It's a
powerful blessing He has designed
to share with us.

The Help We Need

There are some problems people just can't solve. Not everything has a quick and easy solution. Yet even the seemingly unsolvable problems are not hopeless. There is One larger than all humankind who has solutions people would never think to try. When everything else has failed, He is waiting to provide the help we need.

God Values Our Love

When we love someone, we want
to be with them, and we view their
love for us with great honor even
if they are not a person of great
rank—God values our love.
So much, in fact, that He suffered
greatly on our behalf.

JOHN CHRYSOSTOM

Oneness with God

Jesus Christ reconciled the human race, putting it back to where God designed it to be. And now anyone can experience that reconciliation, being brought into oneness with God, on the basis of what our Lord has done on the cross.

OSWALD CHAMBERS

Wonderful Father

For [God] is indeed a wonderful
Father who longs to pour out His
mercy upon us, and whose majesty
is so great He can transform us
from deep within.

TERESA OF AVILA

Be Anxious for Nothing

Be anxious for nothing, but
in everything by prayer and
supplication, with thanksgiving,
let your requests be made known
to God; and the peace of God,
which surpasses all understanding,
will guard your hearts and minds
through Christ Jesus.

PHILIPPIANS 4:6–7 NKJV

Immortal

Our Creator would never have
made such lovely days, and have
given us the deep hearts to enjoy
them, above and beyond all
thought, unless we were meant to
be immortal.

NATHANIEL HAWTHORNE

River of Grace

The river of Thy grace
is flowing free;
We launch upon its
depths to sail to Thee.
In the ocean of Thy
love we soon shall be;
We are sailing to eternity.

PAUL RADER

The Good Shepherd

Is any name more comforting to weary, needy children of our God than Jesus' name of Shepherd? Feeding, leading beside the still water, watching over all our wanderings, bringing us. . .out of the wilderness over the Jordan into the land of peace of plenty.

CHARLES E. HURLBURT AND T. C. HORTON

Equality

Bring us, O Lord God. . .to enter
into that gate and dwell in that
house, where there shall be no
darkness nor dazzling, but one
equal light; no noise nor silence,
but one equal music. . .no ends or
beginnings, but one equal eternity;
in the habitations of Your majesty
and Your glory, world without end.

JOHN DONNE

Redemption

As redemption creates the life of God in us, it also creates the things which belong to that life. The only thing that can possibly satisfy the need is what created the need. This is the meaning of redemption—it creates and it satisfies.

OSWALD CHAMBERS

Against His Heart

God's holy beauty comes near you,
like a spiritual scent, and it stirs
your drowsing soul. . . . He creates
in you the desire to find Him
and run after Him—to follow
wherever He leads you, and to
press peacefully against His heart
wherever He is.

JOHN OF THE CROSS

On Him Alone

Let us begin from this moment to acknowledge Him in all our ways, and do everything, whatsoever we do, as service to Him and for His glory, depending upon Him alone for wisdom, and strength, and sweetness, and patience.

Miracles of Nature

The miracles of nature do not
seem miracles because they are so
common. If no one had ever seen
a flower, even a dandelion would
be the most startling event in the
world.

UNKNOWN

Daily Blessings

The sun. . .in its full glory,
either at rising or setting—this
and many other like blessings
we enjoy daily; and for the most
of them, because they are so
common, most men forget to pay
their praises. But let not us.

IZAAK WALTON

Jesus Makes Me Whole

Jesus, I am resting, resting in the
  joy of what Thou art;
I am finding out the greatness of
  Thy loving heart.
Thou hast bid me gaze upon Thee,
and Thy beauty fills my soul,
For by Thy transforming power,
Thou hast made me whole.

JEAN SOPHIA PIGOTT

Nothing Surprises God

Need strength? Look to Jesus.
Are you confused, hurting,
doubtful? Any emotion you feel,
He can relate to. During His years
on earth, He learned about them
all. Nothing comes as a surprise to
Him. Whatever we face, God wants
to share His strength with us.

God Never Quits

No Christian is beyond God's
grace and peace. . . . Jesus picks up
fallen people with His unending
grace and mercy. He never, never,
never gives up on a child who calls
out to Him.

Eternity

Christians know what it means to
suffer for a while to get something
even better. Today we go through
some troubles; some believers even
die for their faithful testimony.
Why do we put up with such
things? Because we look forward
to something much better—our
eyes focus on eternity with Jesus.

A Good Friend

A really good friend—the kind
Jesus wants to create—can be hard
to find. It takes commitment to a
person's best interests to stir that
person up to love and good works,
and it needs to be done gently if
it's going to work. Be that kind
of person who gently stirs up love
and good works. Then God, who
is Best Friend to you both, will be
pleased.

His Majesty and Power

Reaping the benefits of righteous living is not simply a result of our efforts. Apart from Jesus, the glorious One with authority over the world—and our lives—it never could have happened. Let's glorify His majesty and power again.

Everlasting

Do you not know? Have you not heard? The LORD is the everlasting God, the Creator of the ends of the earth. He will not grow tired or weary, and his understanding no one can fathom. He gives strength to the weary and increases the power of the weak.

ISAIAH 40:28–29 NIV

A Lifeline

If we believe in Jesus, we've been
cast a lifeline. We've connected
ourselves to Him in faith,
and though we struggle to work
out our beliefs with consistency,
our hearts are truly His. That
internal confidence earned us the
greatest reward; eternity with our
Savior.

Reflect His Glory

As sin begins to lose its grip,
our lives increasingly reflect His
glory. We stumble less and reap
the benefits of righteous living
as our lives please both God and
ourselves. The pain of sin has less
and less impact on us, and our
hearts are filled with joy.

Faith in Jesus Lasts Forever

There's nothing wrong with
having a healthy degree of self-
confidence. In fact, building your
faith may also build up your ability
to think properly of yourself.
But no matter how many social
skills you develop, don't trust in
them alone. Because everything
they offer will be here today and
gone in eternity. Only faith in
Jesus lasts forever.

The Love of God

May the God of love and peace set
your heart at rest and speed you on
your journey. May He meanwhile
shelter you from disturbance by
others in the place of complete
plentitude where you will repose
forever in the vision of peace,
in the security of trust, and in the
restful enjoyment of His riches.

RAYMOND OF PENYAFORT

God Is the Journey

Shine forth in splendor,
Thou that art calm weather, and
a quiet resting place for faithful
souls. To see Thee is the end and
the beginning, Thou carriest us,
and Thou dost go before; Thou art
the journey, and the journey's end.

BOETHIUS

Angels

There is singing up in heaven
  such as we have never known,
Where the angels sing the praises
  of the Lamb upon the throne;
Their sweet harps are always
  tuneful and their voices
  always clear.
O, that we might be more like
  them as we serve
  the Master here.

JOHNSON OATMAN JR.

A Thankful Hearth

Let the thankful heart sweep through the day, and, as the magnet finds the iron, so it will find in every hour some heavenly blessing; only the iron in God's hand is gold.

HENRY WARD BEECHER

Unexpected Supplies

"Amplius" means broader, fuller, wider. That is God's perpetual word to us in relation to the filling of the Holy Spirit. We can never have enough to satisfy His yearning desire. When we have apprehended most, there are always unexpected supplies in store ready to be drawn upon.

F. B. MEYER

Call Out to Him

Struggling with a besetting sin? Don't give up. God hasn't. The glorious Savior is working within to bring you into His way. Today you may stumble less than before, and years from now, this temptation may lose its hold on you. We never walk alone when temptation threatens. Jesus is nearby, waiting to help, if only we call out to Him.

Ebb and Flow

When we offer mercy to others, not only does God approve, people often recognize the good we've done and are more likely to give us a break, too. This ebb and flow of mercy is just what God had in mind. Mercy, passed around the world by kindhearted Christians, changes a lot of attitudes and hearts.

June 27/10

God's Design

What a delightful picture of a
faithful person: a well-watered tree
that never drops its leaves. It's easy
to imagine a large tree, spreading
wide and bearing plentifully. God's
design is that we be like that tree,
sending our roots deep into life
and finding prosperity.

Share the Love

Has Jesus comforted you? Pass on
what you received. Suffering ones
yearn to hear that God has aided
others and will also help them.
You can tell them His promises
are as true today as they were when
He spoke them. As you share the
blessing, God will also bless you.
It's always a joy to tell of the love
of Jesus.

Challenge

If we have been faithful, let us
challenge ourselves to become
more so. And if we doubt that
God has made us prosper,
let us consider what prosperity
means. Are we looking for more
money and a bigger car or deeper
faithfulness to Him? Which will
shine brighter in eternity—the
polish on that car or a life that
gleams for Him?

Proven Promise

Those who have experienced
mourning with Jesus by their side
can attest to the truth of His
claim. Anyone who has never
mourned and felt the constant,
faithful support of this Best
Friend cannot appreciate the good
that comes from mourning—the
proved trust that Jesus will always
be faithful. Those who have felt
the arm of the Lord around them
in sorrow have proved this promise
again and again.

The Path of Peace

"Praise be to the Lord, the God of
Israel, because he has come and
has redeemed his people. . .
because of the tender mercy of our
God, by which the rising sun will
come to us from heaven to shine
on those living in darkness and in
the shadow of death, to guide our
feet into the path of peace."

LUKE 1:68, 78–79 NIV

He Will Carry You

"Listen to me. . .you whom I have
upheld since you were conceived,
and have carried since your birth.
Even to your old age and gray
hairs I am he, I am he who will
sustain you. I have made you and I
will carry you."

ISAIAH 46:3–4 NIV

A Supernatural Grandeur

Prayer is an upward leap of the heart, an untroubled glance toward heaven, a cry of gratitude and love which I utter from the depths of sorrow as well as from the heights of joy. It has a supernatural grandeur that expands the soul and unites it with God.

ST. TERESE OF LISIEUX

In Hearts of Men

Jesus shut within a book
   isn't worth a passing look.
Jesus prisoned in a creed
   is a fruitless Lord indeed.
But Jesus in the hearts of men
   shows His tenderness again.

Father of All

It is right and good that we, for all things, at all times, and in all places, give thanks and praise to You, O God. We worship You, we confess to You, we praise You, we bless You, we sing to You, and we give thanks to You: Maker, Nourisher, Guardian, Healer, Lord, and Father of all.

God's Filling

Those who recognize their own
emptiness, then turn to Jesus and
are filled with His Spirit, are given
a new life. Eventually they inherit
heaven with Him. But from that
first breath of new life, heaven
lies within their hearts, and God's
filling has begun.

God's Will

It is God's will that we believe that
we see Him continually, though it
seems to us that the sight be only
partial; and through this belief
He makes us always to gain more
grace, for God wishes to be seen,
and He wishes to be sought,
and He wishes to be expected, and
He wishes to be trusted.

JULIAN OF NORWICH

Brief Temptation

As Christians we've taken part in a
change of ownership that so brings
God into our daily lives that His
enemy makes no more than a brief
temptation call on us, instead of
sitting down in our parlor and
making himself at home.

Little Flower

Flower in the crannied wall,
I pluck you out of the crannies,
I hold you here, root and all,
   in my hand,
Little Flower—but if
   I could understand
What you are, root and all,
   and all in all,
I would know what God and man is.

ALFRED LORD TENNYSON

Just in Time

When we look back at our lives,
will we view a life of thanks for
gifts God sent quickly, barely
in time, or incredibly slowly,
in our opinion? Whether we
merely asked, sought, or knocked
incessantly, at the end of our
lives we'll certainly realize that
everything came just in time—
God's time. And our praises will
ring through all the earth.

Overflowing Compassion

One huge, aching void, a collection of unmet needs. . . present a problem to us or any human. But to Jesus, they are an opportunity to fill us with His love. Where we cannot forgive, He can empty those closets filled with fear and doubt and replace them with overflowing compassion.

Stand Firm

As we remain faithful in the
face of temptation and trust that
God will keep His promises, God
begins to work. Small changes in
our spiritual lives may have larger
ones in His kingdom, as we stand
firm in the faith. In the end, when
we reach heaven, we'll clearly see
the impact of faithfulness. . . .

Moments of His Grace

God's grace is too big, too great
to understand fully. So we
must take the moments of His
grace throughout the day with us:
the music of the songbird in the
morning, the kindness shown in
the afternoon, and the restful
sleep at night.

ANONYMOUS

Thou Alone

Come, my Light, and illumine
my darkness. Come, my Life,
and revive me from death. . . .
Come, my Flame of divine love,
and burn up the thorns of my sins,
kindling my heart with the flame
of Thy love. Come, my King, sit
upon the throne of my heart and
reign there. For Thou alone art my
King and my Lord.

DIMITRI OF ROSTOV

The Surest Way to Happiness

If anyone would tell you the shortest, surest way to happiness and all perfection, he must tell to make it a rule to yourself to thank and praise God for everything that happens to you. For it is certain that whatever seeming calamity happens to you, if you thank and praise God for it, you turn it into a blessing.

WILLIAM LAW

Share with Others

Through Jesus, therefore, let
us continually offer to God a
sacrifice of praise—the fruit of
lips that confess his name.
And do not forget to do good and
to share with others, for with such
sacrifices God is pleased.

HEBREWS 13:15–16 NIV

No Need Is Too Small

Gratitude consists in a watchful, minute attention to the particulars of our state and to the multitude of God's gifts, taken one by one. It fills us with a consciousness that God loves and cares for us, even to the least event and smallest need of life.

HENRY EDWARD MANNING

Measure of Need

Jesus Christ, our Great High
Priest, not only has a great
compassion in His heart, but. . .
He has a special and a particular
compassion measured out
according to every individual
man's measure of need, according
to every individual man's specialty
and particularity and singularity
and secrecy of need.

THOMAS GOODWIN

Equal Glory

I know that He who is far outside
the whole creation takes me within
Himself and hides me in His
arms. . . . He is in my heart, He is
in heaven: Both there and here He
shows Himself to me with equal
glory.

SYMEON THE NEW THEOLOGIAN

Our Real Home

Keeping God's Word may cost
something today, but the price
will never compare with unending
benefits in an eternity of salvation.
So when we struggle to keep our
faith on track, trust fully in all
Jesus said, and live consistently
with the scriptures, let's remind
ourselves where we're heading:
Heaven is our real home.

Wonderful Answers

When we hope for an awesome
response to our communication
with God, it's not because we're
so wonderful. Finding the perfect
way to ask won't work—that's
expecting magic, not faith.
But somehow, as we do ordinary
petitioning, God provides the
wonderful answers.

Great Promise of Eternal Life

Jesus wants those whose hearts,
minds, and spirits are engaged
with Him and willing to act on His
words. Those who do that receive
a great promise—eternal life,
uncounted ages in which to draw
even nearer to the One whose
Word meant so much in earthly
life.

The Gift

Like any other gift, the gift of
grace can be yours only if you'll
reach out and take it. Maybe being
about to reach out and take it is a
gift, too.

FREDERICK BUECHNER

Glory in This. . .

Thus saith the LORD, Let not the
wise man glory in his wisdom,
neither let the mighty man glory
in his might, let not the rich man
glory in his riches: but let him
that glorieth glory in this, that he
understandeth and knoweth me,
that I am the LORD which exercise
lovingkindness, judgment, and
righteousness, in the earth: for in
these things I delight.

JEREMIAH 9:23–24 KJV

The Right Things

Though the last battle may be long off, destruction is the ultimate end for those who hate God. But strength given to believers allows them to fight on when the enemy seems strong. Blessings are the reinforcements that enable us when the battle becomes hard. God always gives the right things to the right people—those who trust in Him.

You Can't Help but Grow

All the stretching and pulling in the world could not make a dead oak grow; but a live oak grows without stretching. The essential thing is to get within you the growing life, and you cannot help but grow.

Service

Service of any sort becomes
delightful to the soul; having
surrendered its will into the
keeping of the Lord, the soul finds
itself really wanting to do the
things God wants it to do.

Joy Unspeakable

Joy improves our personalities,
increases our energy, transforms
our worship, and bears us through
difficulties. It is joy unspeakable
and full of glory.

ROBERT J. MORGAN

Deliverance in Faith

There is deliverance in the
wonderful life of faith. For in
this life no burdens are carried,
no anxieties felt. The Lord is our
burden-bearer, and upon Him we
must lay off every care.

In Our Hearts. . .

Sometimes our thoughts turn back
toward a corner in a forest, or
the end of a bank, or an orchard
filled with flowers, seen but a
single time. . .yet remaining in our
hearts. . .a feeling [we] have just
passed by happiness.

GUY DE MAUPASSANT

Sing for Joy!

"Let the heavens rejoice, let the
earth be glad; let them say among
the nations, "The LORD reigns!"
Let the sea resound, and all that is
in it; let the fields be jubilant, and
everything in them! Then the trees
of the forest will sing, they will
sing for joy before the LORD, for
he comes to judge the earth. Give
thanks to the LORD, for he is good;
his love endures forever."

1 CHRONICLES 16:31–34 NIV

Every Minute

Happiness cannot be traveled
to, owned, earned, worn, or
consumed. Happiness is the
spiritual experience of living
every minute with love, grace, and
gratitude.

Denis Waitley

Effectual Workers

The most effectual workers I know
are those who do not feel the least
care or anxiety about their work,
but who commit it all to their dear
Master and trust Him implicitly
for each moment's needed supplies
of wisdom and strength.

At His Right Hand

He raised [Christ] from the dead
and seated him at his right hand
in the heavenly realms, far above
all rule and authority, power and
dominion, and every title that can
be given, not only in the present
age but also in the one to come.

EPHESIANS 1:20–21 NIV

Grace Makes the
Soul Comfortable

Grace is no stationary thing,
it is ever becoming. It is flowing
straight out of God's heart.
Grace does nothing but re-form
and convey God. Grace makes the
soul comfortable to the will of
God. God, the ground of the soul,
and grace go together.

MEISTER ECKHART

Let Your Light Shine

Let Jesus be in your heart,
Eternity in your spirit,
The world under your feet,
The will of God in your actions.
And let the love of God shine
forth from you.

CATHERINE OF GENOA

Rest in God

The thought of You stirs us so
deeply that we cannot be content
unless we praise You, because You
have made us for Yourself and our
hearts find no peace until they rest
in You.

St. Augustine

Joy-Bearer

To be a joy-bearer and a joy-giver
says everything, for in our life,
if one is joyful, it means that one
is faithfully living for God, and
that nothing else counts; and if
one gives joy to others one is doing
God's work; with joy without and
joy within, all is well.

JANET ERSKINE STUART

Ideals

Ideals are like stars; you will not
succeed in touching them with
your hands. But like the seafaring
man on the desert of waters,
you choose them as your guides,
and following them you will
reach your destiny.

CARL SCHURZ

Our Protection

Human effort never fully defends us from harm. Storms come and damage our land. Terrorists attack. Only one Protector keeps us really safe, whether it's from physical harm, emotional hurt, or a spiritual temptation. Only One aids us in pain, day or night. Jesus is true protection from trouble and a companion in every trial. He'll stand by us faithfully.

Cling to Jesus

Whether we are joyful or sad,
God still remains faithful. He
provides for our needs, even if we
don't get the lavish things we'd
prefer. And He always provides
generous spiritual blessings for
those who trust in Him. No matter
what your circumstances, you can
always cling to Jesus—and be
blessed.

As Gentle Rain

The quality of mercy
  is not strain'd,
It droppeth as the gentle rain
  from heaven
Upon the place beneath.
  It is twice blessed:
It blesseth him that gives,
  and him that takes.

WILLIAM SHAKESPEARE

At Home in Christ

People find themselves "homeless" in many ways. In fact, we all more or less are that way from the day we're born. Until we come to [God] in faith, we wander in a desert of false religion and self-sufficiency. God created us to be at home in Him.

Don't Despair

Jesus revels in believers.
God doesn't save anyone whom He
does not consistently delight in.
On those days when you're faithful
but unfulfilled, feeling miserable
and unloved, don't despair.
Jesus is rejoicing with you,
comforting you, and singing
joyfully at your faithful service to
Him. He always rejoices in His
faithful ones.

Better and Brighter Moments

Trust that God will help you work
things out, and that all the unclear
moments will bring you to that
moment of clarity and action
when you are known by Him and
know Him. These are the better
and brighter moments of His
blessing.

God Is Everywhere

There's not a tint
   that paints the rose
Or decks the lily fair,
Or marks the humblest
   flower that grows,
But God has placed it there. . . .
There's not a place
   on earth's vast round,
In ocean's deep or air,
Where love and beauty
   are not found,
For God is everywhere.

JAMES C. WALLACE

Everything Is God's

Yours, O LORD, is the greatness
and the power and the glory and
the majesty and the splendor,
for everything in heaven and earth
is yours. Yours, O LORD, is the
kingdom; you are exalted as head
over all. . . . In your hands are
strength and power to exalt and
give strength to all.

1 CHRONICLES 29:11–12 NIV

To Succeed

To appreciate beauty; to find the
best in others; to give one's self;
to leave the world a little better,
whether by a healthy child,
a garden patch, or a redeemed
social condition; to have played
and laughed with enthusiasm,
and sung with exultation; to know
even one life has breathed easier
because you have lived. . . . This is
to have succeeded.

RALPH WALDO EMERSON

God Is Infinite

God is infinite in His simplicity
and simple in His infinity.
Therefore He is everywhere
and is everywhere complete.
He is everywhere on account of
His infinity and is everywhere
complete on account of His
simplicity.

MEISTER ECKHART

To Life Eternal

May God bestow on us His grace
With blessings rich provide us,
And may the brightness
 of His face
To life eternal guide us.

Martin Luther

The Soul Is a Temple

The soul is a temple, and God
is silently building it by night
and by day. Precious thoughts
are building it, unselfish love is
building it; all-penetrating faith is
building it.

HENRY WARD BEECHER

God's Love Is Perfect

Love gone wrong can dry out your
soul. It's not the love this world
was founded on, so it can never
give us what we need. But there's
one love that every person, weak or
strong, can enjoy. It won't lead to
a bad place or break a heart. God's
love is perfect.

God's Timing Is Perfect

Time may drag as you're waiting for God to aid you in a difficult situation. You begin to wonder if He'll ever intervene. Then when you least expect it, He brings wonderful change into your life. Is God slow? No, He just has another plan, and when the time is perfect, He does what you need.

His Grace Is Sufficient

[The Lord] told me, "My grace
is enough; it's all you need. My
strength comes into its own in
your weakness." Once I heard that,
I was glad to let it happen.
I quit focusing on the handicap
and began appreciating the gift.
It was a case of Christ's strength
moving in on my weakness.

2 CORINTHIANS 12:9 MSG

'Tis So Sweet

'Tis so sweet to trust in Jesus,
And to take Him at His word:
Just to rest upon His promise,
And to know, "Thus says the
Lord!"

LOUISA M. R. STEAD

God's Divine Gift

Love. What is love?
  No one can define it;
It's something so great,
  only God could design it.
Yes, love is beyond
  what man can define,
For love is immortal,
  and God's gift is divine.

UNKNOWN

God's Victory

Pure gold put in the fire comes out
of it *proved* pure; genuine faith put
through this suffering comes out
proved genuine. When Jesus wraps
this all up, it's your faith, not your
gold, that God will have on display
as evidence of his victory.

1 PETER 1:7 MSG

Daily Guidance

Lay the burden of your work on
the Lord. The result is a happy
pathway of daily guidance in which
you are led into much blessed work
for your Master and ability to do
it all without a care or a burden
because He prepares the way
before you.

Spreading His Light

Free of the need to secure a
place in eternity, we can devote
ourselves to spreading His light,
selflessly sharing the way to the
Father whose gift means all to
us. Set high above the earn-your-
way-into-heaven crowd, we shine
brightly and light the path to Jesus.

A Love Relationship

Had God left us to earn our
own salvation, we'd be truly
desperate. We couldn't be the
light of the world that He calls
us to be. But when we recognize
that He controls all the world
and that our hearts are part of it,
when we submit ourselves to His
will instead of finding our own
solutions, His Spirit leads us in
a love relationship that changes
hearts and minds.

Leave Them with God

Never indulge, at the close of
an action, in any self-reflective
acts of any kind, whether self-
congratulation or of self-despair.
Forget the things which are behind
the moment they are past, leaving
them with God.

Humble

"If my people, who are called by my name, will humble themselves and pray and seek my face and turn from their wicked ways, then will I hear from heaven and will forgive their sin and will heal their land."

2 CHRONICLES 7:14 NIV

I Am. . .

I am not what I ought to be. I am
not what I wish to be. I am not
even what I hope to be. But by the
cross of Christ, I am not what I
was.

JOHN NEWTON

Praise Him

Praise him, all his angels,
praise him, all his heavenly hosts.
Praise him, sun and moon, praise
him, all you shining stars. Praise
him, you highest heavens and you
waters above the skies. Let them
praise the name of the LORD, for
he commanded and they were
created. He set them in place for
ever and ever; he gave a decree that
will never pass away.

PSALM 148:2–6 NIV

Nothing Wanting

The Bible is one of the greatest blessings bestowed by God on the children of men. It has God for its author, salvation for its end, and truth without any mixture for its matter. It is all pure, all sincere; nothing too much; nothing wanting.

JOHN LOCKE

Renewed

By reading the scriptures I am
so renewed that all nature seems
renewed around me and with
me. The sky seems to be a pure,
a cooler blue, the trees a deeper
green. . . . The whole world is
charged with the glory of God and
I feel fire and music. . .under my
feet.

THOMAS MERTON

Christ

In His life, Christ is an example, showing us how to live; in His death, He is a sacrifice, satisfying for our sins; in His resurrection, a conqueror; in His ascension, a king; in His intercession, a high priest.

MARTIN LUTHER

Woven into Jesus

God will never, never, never let
us down if we have faith and put
our trust in Him. He will always
look after us. So we must cleave to
Jesus. Our whole life must simply
be woven into Jesus.

MOTHER TERESA

Three Little Words

These three little words repeated
over and over, "Jesus saves me,
Jesus saves me," will put to flight
the greatest of doubts that ever
assaulted any soul.

He Is Praying

If I could hear Christ praying
for me in the next room, I would
not fear a million enemies.
Yet distance makes no difference.
He is praying for me.

ROBERT MURRAY MCCHEYNE

Fruit

The Divine Husbandman who has
the care of the vine will care also
for you who are His branches and
will so prune and purge and water
and tend you that you will grow
and bring forth fruit.

Praise God for Himself

Although it be good to think upon
the kindness of God, and to love
Him and praise Him for it; yet it
is far better to gaze upon the pure
essence of Him and to love Him
and praise Him for Himself.

Sleep in Peace

Have courage for the great
sorrows of life and patience for
the small ones; and when you have
laboriously accomplished your
daily task, go to sleep in peace.
God is awake.

VICTOR HUGO

Nature Is a Treasure

If we are children of God, we have a tremendous treasure in nature and will realize that it is holy and sacred. We will see God reaching out to us in every wind that blows, every sunrise and sunset, every cloud in the sky, every flower that blooms, and every leaf that fades.

OSWALD CHAMBERS

Precious

How precious He is! The more
we know about Him the more
wonderful He becomes, and the
more intimately we know Him the
more precious He is. . . . He holds
the world in the hollow of His
hand as a dry leaf and could crush
it. But He so loved you and me
that He laid aside His royal robe,
arrayed Himself in human flesh,
and then poured out His precious
blood for us.

CHARLES E. HURLBURT AND T. C. HORTON

The Holy Fire

Joy is the holy fire that keeps our
purpose warm and our intelligence
aglow. Work without joy is
nothing. Resolve to keep happy,
and your joy and you shall form an
invincible host against difficulties.

HELEN KELLER

As Dust

All the joy and delight, all the
pleasures a thousand worlds could
offer, are as dust in the balance
when weighed against one hour of
this mutual exchange of love and
communion with the Lord.

CORA HARRIS MACILRAVY

Have You Not Heard?

Have you not known? Have you
not heard? The everlasting God,
the LORD, the Creator of the ends
of the earth, neither faints nor
is weary. His understanding is
unsearchable.

ISAIAH 40:28 NKJV

Available Blessings

God's blessings are available to
even the most disobedient child
who turns from sin. Pray for that
loved one to turn and accept the
Savior's love. Over and over God
gave that blessing to Israel.
He'll give it to those you love, too.

God's Will

True friendship with God. . .means
being so intimately in touch with
God that you never even need to
ask Him to show you His will.
You are God's will. And all of your
seemingly commonsense decisions
are actually His will for you,
unless you sense a check in your
spirit.

OSWALD CHAMBERS

He Will Never Fail

If we don't see God's compassions,
perhaps we've been blinded by our
situation. But no event on earth
changes His tender care for us.
All we need is trusting faith that
He will never fail. And He won't.

Ways to Share

God's works are so wonderful,
sometimes we can hardly contain
them. Other times, that flame
burns a little lower. But the Lord
always provides us with ways to
share our faith.

God Doesn't Alter

God doesn't alter. What He was
when the prophet Jeremiah wrote,
"His compassions fail not," is what
He still is. No word of scripture
has changed since He first inspired
it—the story of His faithfulness
remains the same from age to age.

God's Intention

Abundant life, full of good
things on this earth, spiritual
peace and joy, and full, satisfying
relationships—that's what God
intends His people to have.
Because Jesus entered your life,
you've entered a new realm.
Life has taken on a new meaning
because you know the Creator.

Perseverance

Consider it pure joy, my brothers,
whenever you face trials of many
kinds, because you know that
the testing of your faith develops
perseverance. Perseverance must
finish its work so that you may be
mature and complete, not lacking
anything.

JAMES 1:2–4 NIV

God Is Faithful

As you wake to a new day of doubt
and questioning, [God's] new
compassions are ready to meet
you. They cannot disappear or fail
you, because He promised they
will be there, and for that not to be
true would mean that God became
faithless. God's faithful nature
never changes.

Joy That Doesn't Stop

Because you know the Creator,
you feel clean, right with your
Maker, and richer for being in a
relationship with Him. Though
you're far from perfect,
He's been working in your life to
bring spiritual abundance, deeper
understanding of Him and the
world around you, and a joy that
doesn't stop when trouble enters
the door.

When Trouble Hits. . .

When trouble hits, people often
start asking questions. *Where is
God?* they wonder when a family
member becomes seriously ill or
a war starts. It's normal to feel
confusion for a while when you're
hit with large problems. But as
you enter that time of confusion,
be sure of one thing: God has not
deserted you.

My Treasure

Riches I heed not, nor man's
empty praise, Thou mine
inheritance, now and always:
Thou and Thou only, first in my
heart, High King of heaven, my
treasure Thou art.

CELTIC TRADITIONAL

The Promise Is Yours

Sometimes we forget to let God be the source of strength in our lives. We think we must do it all ourselves. Lord, remind us to never doubt the salvation You promised us. We march toward a better place.

Open Your Door to God

We throw open our doors to God and discover at the same moment that he has already thrown open his door to us. We find ourselves standing where we always hoped we might stand—out in the wide open spaces of God's grace and glory, standing tall and shouting our praise.

ROMANS 5:2 MSG

What Greater Happiness

It is good to be with Jesus and to remain here forever. What greater happiness or higher honor could we have than to be with God, to be made like Him and to live in His light?

ANASTASIUS OF SINAI

Limitless Hope

When we take time to notice the simple things in life, we never lack for encouragement. We discover we are surrounded by limitless hope that's just wearing everyday clothes.

ANONYMOUS

The Way

Without the Way,
There is no going;
Without the Truth,
There is no knowing;
Without the Life,
There is no living.

THOMAS À KEMPIS

What Is Grace?

What is grace? It is the inspiration from on high; it is love; it is liberty. Grace is the spirit of law. This discovery of the spirit belongs to Saint Paul, and what he calls "grace" from a heavenly point of view, we, from an earthly point, call "righteousness."

VICTOR HUGO

Bright Crystals

The world is so full of care and
sorrow that it is a gracious debt we
owe to one another to discover the
bright crystals of delight hidden
in somber circumstances and
irksome tasks.

HELEN KELLER

Happiness

Happiness consists more in small conveniences or pleasures that occur every day, than in great pieces of good fortune that happen but seldom to a man in the course of his life.

BENJAMIN FRANKLIN

Take Notice

The wonderful thing about sunset,
and much the same can be said
for sunrise, is that it happens
every day; and even if the sunset
itself is not spectacular, it marks
the beginning of another day.
It's a great time to pause and take
notice.

ELAINE ST. JAMES

Thank You, God

I thank You, God, for this most
amazing day, for the leaping
greenly spirits of trees, and for
the blue dream of sky and for
everything which is natural,
which is infinite, which is yes.

E. E. Cummings

Those Who Love

Those who love are borne on wings;
they run and are filled with joy;
they are free and unrestricted. . . .
Beyond all things they rest in the
one highest thing, from whom
streams all that is good.

THOMAS À KEMPIS

Secure

And none shall pluck us
  from that hand.
Eternally we are secure.
Though heaven and earth
  shall pass away,
[God's] Word forever shall endure.

MRS. M. E. RAE

Believe. . .

Faith is the root of all blessings.
Believe and you shall be saved;
believe and your needs must be
satisfied; believe and you cannot
but be comforted and happy.

JEREMY TAYLOR

In Order

To put the world in order, we must
first put the nation in order.
To put the nation in order, we
must first put the family in order.
To put the family in order, we
must first cultivate our personal
life. And to cultivate our personal
life, we must set our hearts right.

CONFUCIUS

Love

Love bore our sins away;
Love gave us life anew;
Love opened wide
  the gates of heaven;
Love gave us work to do.

RUTH A. ATWELL

The Wonder of Living

The wonder of living is held
within the beauty of silence,
the glory of sunlight, the sweetness
of fresh spring air, the quiet
strength of earth, and the love that
lies at the very root of all things.

ANONYMOUS

Pure and Lovely

The things we think on are the
things that feed our souls. If we
think on pure and lovely things,
we shall grow pure and lovely like
them.

Happiness of Life

The happiness of life is made up
of minute fractions—the little,
soon-forgotten charities of a
kiss or a smile, a kind look or a
heartfelt compliment.

SAMUEL TAYLOR COLERIDGE

A Living Hope

Praise be to the God and Father of our Lord Jesus Christ! In his great mercy he has given us new birth into a living hope through the resurrection of Jesus Christ from the dead, and into an inheritance that can never perish, spoil or fade—kept in heaven for you, who through faith are shielded by God's power. . . . In this you greatly rejoice.

1 PETER 1:3–6 NIV

True Nature of Things

For in the true nature of things,
if we will rightly consider,
every green tree is far more
glorious than if it were made
of gold and silver.

MARTIN LUTHER

God Gives Us Grace

God, give us grace to accept with serenity the things that cannot be changed, courage to change the things that can be changed, and the wisdom to distinguish one from another.

REINHOLD NIEBUHR

No Limits

His love has no limits, His grace
has no measure, His power no
boundary known unto men;
For out of His infinite riches in
Jesus He giveth, and giveth,
and giveth again.

ANNIE J. FLINT

The Power of Prayer

We know the power of prayer.
What greater need could we have,
than to have God guide our steps
as we near the end of history?
With His impact on our lives,
whether He tarries one day or a
thousand years, we are ready.

Fountain of Grace

Fountain of grace, rich,
　full and free,
What need I, that is not in Thee?
Full pardon, strength
　to meet the day,
And peace which none
　　can take away.

JAMES EDMESTON

The Sweetest Things in Life

The best things are nearest; breath
in your nostrils, light in your eyes,
flowers at your feet, duties at your
hand, the path of Right just before
you. Do not grasp at the stars,
but do life's plain common work as
it comes, certain that daily duties
and daily bread are the sweetest
things in life.

ROBERT LOUIS STEVENSON

Things Will Flow

As your faith is strengthened you
will find that there is no longer the
need to have a sense of control,
that things will flow as they will,
and that you will flow with them,
to your great delight and benefit.

EMMANUEL TENEY

It's Beautiful!

How beautiful it is to be alive!
  To wake each morn as if
  the Maker's grace
Did us a fresh from
  nothing derive,
That we might sing "How happy is
  our case! How beautiful
  it is to be alive!"

HENRY SEPTIMUS SUTTON

The Wondrous Plan

Grace, 'tis a charming sound,
Harmonious to mine ear;
Heaven with the echo
   shall resound,
And all the earth shall hear.
Grace first contrived the way
To save rebellious man;
And all the steps that grace display
Which drew a wondrous plan.

PHILIP DODDRIDGE

Run If We Must

Half the joy of life is in little
things taken on the run. Let us
run if we must. . .but let us keep
our hearts young and our eyes
open that nothing worth our while
shall escape us. And everything is
worth its while if we only grasp it
and its significance.

CHARLES VICTOR CHERBULIEZ

WHISPERS OF
Promise

You Are a Part

You are part of the great plan,
an indispensable part. You are
needed; you have your own unique
share in the freedom of creation.

MADELEINE L'ENGLE

The Best Thing to Give

The best thing to give to your
enemy is forgiveness; to an
opponent, tolerance; to a friend,
your heart; to your child, a good
example. . .to yourself, respect; to
all. . .charity.

LORD BALFOUR

Splendor

The splendor of the rose and the whiteness of the lily do not rob the little violet of its scent nor the daisy of its simple charm. If every tiny flower wanted to be a rose, spring would lose its loveliness.

THÉRÈSE OF LISIEUX

Respect

Reverently respect GOD, your God,
serve him, hold tight to him. . . .
He's your praise! He's your God!
He did all these tremendous, these
staggering things that you saw with
your own eyes.

DEUTERONOMY 10:20–21 MSG

Rest. . .

Rest is not idleness, and to lie
sometimes on the grass under the
trees on a summer's day, listening
to the murmur of the water, or
watching the clouds float across
the sky, is by no means a waste of
time.

JOHN LUBBOCK

Possessions

Unnecessary possessions are unnecessary burdens. If you have them, you have to take care of them! There is great freedom in simplicity of living. It is those who have enough but not too much who are the happiest.

PEACE PILGRIM

Divine Grace

There are many among the
martyrs of my age or younger,
and as weak or weaker than I,
but the Divine Grace that did
not fail them will sustain me.

ROBERT SOUTHWELL

Faith Shines

No coward soul is mine,
No trembler in the world's
    storm-troubled sphere:
    I see heaven's glories shine,
And faith shines equal, arming me
    from fear.

EMILY BRONTË

The Sun Is There

Even in winter, even in the midst
of the storm, the sun is still there.
Somewhere, up above the clouds,
it still shines and warms and pulls
at the life buried deep inside the
brown branches and frozen earth.
The sun is there! Spring will come!
The clouds cannot stay forever.

GLORIA GAITHER

Praise You

O God, great and wonderful,
who has created the heavens,
dwelling in the light and beauty
of it; who has made the earth,
revealing Yourself in every flower
that opens; let not my eyes be
blind to you, neither my heart be
dead, but teach me to praise You,
even as the lark which offers her
song at daybreak.

ISIDORE OF SEVILLE

Beauty of Holiness

Do our lives see the King in His
beauty? Do we grip the fact as we
gaze upon Him it is His will that
we should be changed unto the
same likeness? . . . O Lord,
let every mist and veil that hide
Thy glory be removed, and every
sin be put away, that we may
behold Thee in the beauty of
holiness.

Far Deeper Than Emotion

Your joy in the Lord is to be a far
deeper thing than a mere emotion.
It is to be the joy of knowledge,
of perception, of actual existence.
It is a far gladder thing to be a bird
than only to feel as if you were a
bird, with no actual power of flying
at all.

Jehovah

Jehovah—"The Self-existent One who reveals Himself." Into the wilderness of my lost way He comes to find me and lead me out. Into the desert of my barren life enters Jehovah and makes all the desert a garden. . . . Shall we not bow before His Majesty and worship Jehovah, while we pray for greater grace to receive all the revelation of Himself which He would give?

CHARLES E. HURLBURT AND T. C. HORTON

God Satisfies the Soul

In comparison with this big world, the human heart is only a small thing. Though the world is so large, it is utterly unable to satisfy this tiny heart. Our ever-growing soul and its capacities can be satisfied only in the infinite God.

SADHU SUNDAR SINGH

The Light of His Face

Why should we live up the hill and swathed in the mists, when we might have an unclouded sky and a radiant sun over our heads if we would climb higher and walk in the light of His face?

ALEXANDER MACLAREN

Nothing Can Stop You

The next time you have a bad day,
remember, you're not doing this in
your power, but God's. Ask Him to
cleanse you of all sin, showing you
the way you need to go, and then
start walking. Remember you're
heading toward His glory and
goodness. Nothing can stop you
now.

Know Jesus Thoroughly

One day, each Christian shall
have a different relationship with
the Lord. There will be no gaps
of knowledge. Every believer will
know Jesus thoroughly, just as
He now knows each of us.
We'll be able to fully comprehend
the magnitude of our Savior.

Our Best

What seems our worst prayers
may really be, in God's eyes, our
best. Those, I mean, which are
least supported by devotional
feeling. For these may come from
a deeper level than feeling.
God sometimes seems to speak
to us most intimately when He
catches us, as it were, off our
guard.

C. S. LEWIS

Looking through Glass

While we're here on earth, we still
need to polish up that mirror and
see as clearly as we can who God
is and what He desires of us.
But someday, we know we can look
forward to not having to think
about what God might want—it
will be as clear as looking through
glass, not peering into some
clouded mirror. Then we'll really
know Jesus.

Be Silent

How can you expect God to speak
in that gentle and inward voice
which melts the soul, when you are
making so much noise. . . ?
Be silent and God will speak
again.

FRANÇOIS FÉNELON

All Glory to God

Now all glory to God, who is able
to keep you from falling away and
will bring you with great joy into
his glorious presence without a
single fault. All glory to him who
alone is God, our Savior through
Jesus Christ our Lord. All glory,
majesty, power, and authority
are his before all time, and in
the present, and beyond all time!
Amen.

JUDE 24–25 NLT

God's Faithfulness

If you have years of faithful service to God at your back, you've been through challenges and have seen the loyalty of your Savior. You can testify to another that His peace will come, and the promises will be fulfilled.

Happy to Give

God recognizes that we have
received His forgiveness,
through His Son, and He's happy
to grant us our wishes. He gives
good things that make us happy.
That doesn't mean He gives us
everything we ask for. But when we
ask in Jesus' name, God is happy to
give.

Sweetness

When you're looking for some sweetness in a sour life, turn to scripture. The scriptures are God's huge love letter to His own people. As even the newest believer reads attentively, God's mercy becomes clear. Yet a lifelong believer can read the same passage and see something new again and again.

Harmony

When we pray about everything,
we'll experience two unexpected
benefits: thanksgiving and peace.
We'll appreciate what our Savior
begins to give and offer Him
thanks, deepening and expanding
our trust relationship. As we do
that, harmony will fill our lives.
Find peace in prayer today.

Jesus Cared Enough. . .

God's relationship with the
Christian constantly grows
through His Word, and with it He
shows new depth at every stage of
growth. Don't get caught up in the
mysteries of scripture and miss the
plain, blessed truth of how much
Jesus loves you today. Over and
over, in many ways, He's made it
clear that He cared enough to die
for you.

God Is Interested

God is trying to tell us He wants
to be part of every moment of our
lives—whether it's something we
simply need to mention or a deep
concern we petition for a long
time. He's interested. Only when
we give God all our anxieties can
He have the kind of impact on our
lives that He's always had in mind.

Strength

The same God who guides the stars in their courses, who directs the earth in its orbit, who feeds the burning furnace of the sun and keeps the stars perpetually burning with their fires—the same God has promised to supply thy strength.

CHARLES SPURGEON

Nothing Is Too Small

Maybe we figure we don't need
help with what we're going through
now. But God wants to share good
times, too, and if an unexpected
trouble comes up, He'll be happy
to assist us. Or maybe we think
we don't need to bother God
with something "this small."
But nothing is below the notice
of Him who created subatomic
particles.

God Has Chosen Us

In His mercy God has chosen us,
unworthy as we are, out of this
world to serve Him and thus to
advance in goodness and to bear
the greatest possible purity of love
and patience.

ANTHONY ZACCARIA

God Won't Forget

As we cannot forget our children,
how much less can God erase our
relationship from His memory.
If we, who lack all God's power,
do good things for those we love,
how much more is He willing to
do them for us? All we need do is
trust that something good lies at
the end of this trial—something
God had in mind for us all along.

New-Created

And if tonight my soul may find
her peace in sleep, and sink in
good oblivion, and in the morning
wake like a new-opened flower,
then I have been dipped again in
God, and new-created.

D. H. LAWRENCE

Don't Go Anywhere
without Jesus

Whether you're moving into
new territory or starting a new
ministry, Jesus is at your side.
You can't take on something new
and not have Him by your side. . . .
Don't go anywhere without Jesus.
You don't need to.

Surpassingly Good

There is no situation so chaotic that God cannot, from that situation, create something that is surpassingly good. He did it at the creation. He did it at the cross. He is doing it today.

BISHOP MOULE

The Righteous

But let all who take refuge in you
be glad; let them ever sing for joy.
Spread your protection over them,
that those who love your name
may rejoice in you. For surely, O
LORD, you bless the righteous; you
surround them with your favor as
with a shield.

PSALM 5:11–12 NIV

Daily Bread

He only is the Maker
of all things near and far;
He paints the wayside flower,
He lights the evening star;
The wind and waves obey Him,
by Him the birds are fed;
Much more to us, His children,
He gives our daily bread.

MATTHIAS CLAUDIUS

Born to Deliver

Born Thy people to deliver,
Born a child and yet a king.
Born to reign in us forever,
Now Thy gracious kingdom bring.
By Thine own eternal Spirit
Rule in our hearts alone;
By Thine all sufficient merit,
Raise us to Thy glorious throne.

CHARLES WESLEY

God Governs

I have lived a long time, and the longer I live, the more convincing proof I see of this truth, that God governs in the affairs of men. If a sparrow cannot fall to the ground without His notice, is it probable that an empire can rise without His aid?

BENJAMIN FRANKLIN

Jesus Never Stops

Jesus never stops interceding for us—He's always before the Father, bringing important issues before Him and asking Him to work in our behalf. As our High Priest, His mission is to save us completely.

A Mission

By placing us in this world, God
has given us a mission, and prayer
is part of it. By lifting others up to
Him, we take part in the blessing
He bestows on our world. Just as
Jesus won't forget us, we need to
remember those whose lives we
touch. Because we know Jesus,
we can pray effectively—and
perhaps that's the most important
impact we'll have on another's life.

God Whispers

Each time you pick a daffodil
Or gather violets on some hill
Or touch a leaf or see a tree,
It's all God whispering,
"This is Me."

HELEN STEINER RICE

Christmas Bringeth Jesus

Christmas hath a beauty lovelier
  than the world can show:
For Christmas bringeth Jesus,
  brought for us so low.
Earth, strike up your music,
  birds that sing and bells that ring;
Heaven hath answering music
  for all angels soon to sing:
Earth put on your whitest bridal
  robe of spotless snow:
For Christmas bringeth Jesus;
  brought for us so low.

CHRISTINA ROSSETTI

God Incarnate

Jesus Christ is not the best human being; He is a Being who cannot be accounted for by the human race at all. He is not man becoming God, but God Incarnate, God coming into human flesh, coming into it from outside. His life is the Highest and the Holiest entering in at the lowliest door.

OSWALD CHAMBERS

The Healing Touch

When God cleanses our sin, where
once we could only see scars,
healing begins. Our aching hearts
are covered with the cool, healing
touch of a Savior whose balm
reaches the deepest soul places.
The change has begun. In eternity
we'll see what God now sees—
ourselves entirely cleansed by the
Son, who made us stainless with
His sacrifice.

Friendship

Have you pondered the idea that the Lord of the universe is your friend? Perhaps you've been stopped in your tracks by the awe of that truth. Many blessings follow friendship with God, but so do challenges. The Creator expects much of his friends, just as He gives much.

Praise God for All

Instead of feeling sorry for
ourselves as we advance in years,
or totaling up the days and months
that are already past, let's praise
God for all the benefits He's
already given and look forward to
all those that may lie ahead.

God's Purpose

When the world tempts us to
feel life has passed us by, let's
remember we aren't finished yet.
God may give us many wonderful
relationships, increased spiritual
growth, and physical blessings in
the years ahead. Until our very last
day on earth, God has a purpose
for us here.

Connected to God

Coming to Jesus brings us new
life. Not just a few more years on
earth or a better way of living,
but real, exciting, wonderful life.
Existence free from the necessity
of constant sin. The ability to do
right things for the right reasons.
Life connected to God Himself.

Excellent Things!

Excellent things! God doesn't just do good things or the best things. He does excellent things. What could improve on God's superb plan or will? Are our eyes open to the excellent things He's done for His people—and is still doing for them today?

All the Time

I know Christ dwells within me
all the time, guiding me and
inspiring me whenever I do or
say anything—a light of which I
caught no glimmer before it comes
to me at the very moment when it
is needed.

THÉRÈSE OF LISIEUX

Prince of Peace

For to us a child is born, to us a son is given, and the government will be on his shoulders. And he will be called Wonderful Counselor, Mighty God, Everlasting Father, Prince of Peace.

ISAIAH 9:6 NIV

His Hands

I seem to have been led, little by little, toward my work; and I believe that the same fact will appear in the life of anyone who will cultivate such powers as God has given him, and then go on, bravely, quietly, but persistently, doing such work as comes to his hands.

FANNY CROSBY

"As Gold"

We will all "come forth as gold" (Job 23:10) if we understand that God is sovereign and knows what is best, even when we cannot understand what is happening at the time. He asks us to trust Him and to know that He cares for us even when we can't track Him.

SHIRLEY DOBSON

Evidence

On earth, we may never
comprehend God's desire or plan
to save us, but through the ages, all
Christians have joined in worship
and praise of One who gives so
willingly and generously. We can
certainly rejoice in the results
as we experience overwhelming
evidence of the Savior's love.

Good Things

What a funny place to find good
news—at the end of repentance.
We tend to think of repentance
as a difficult thing, and often it
is, as we struggle to see the world
from God's point of view.
No, repentance is not fun or easy.
But let's remember no really good
things come easily.

God Goes before Us

God faithfully looks out for us,
even when we aren't aware of
problems. Instead of letting us
innocently fall into trouble, He
goes before us and paves the way
to our making the right decision,
as long as we're honestly trying to
follow His will.

Coming to Jesus

The benefit of coming to Jesus
and accepting His salvation is
huge. From sin that entraps us
so we cannot escape, He frees
us in a moment of simple faith.
But God's good gift doesn't free
us from consequences and make
us shallow people who can do
whatever we want and still receive
a blessing. God wants to build us
up in character and make us just
like Him.

Birthday of a King

'Twas a humble birthplace, but
  O how much God gave
  to us that day,
From the manger bed
  what a path has led,
What a perfect, holy way.
Alleluia! O how the angels sang.
Alleluia! How it rang!
And the sky was bright
  with a holy light
'Twas the birthday of a King.

WILLIAM H. NEIDLINGER

God Is in Control

God is still in control of every situation. The universe belongs to Him, including all the people in it. At such a time as this, He may be planning something wonderful a mere step beyond the problem we face. Just because we don't see the blessing yet doesn't mean it isn't on its way.

O Holy Night

O holy night, the stars
  are brightly shining,
It is the night of the
  dear Savior's birth;
Long lay the world
  in sin and error pining,
Till he appeared
  and the soul felt its worth.
A thrill of hope,
  the weary world rejoices,
For yonder breaks
  a new and glorious morn!

JOHN S. DWIGHT

Peace of the World

As evening drew on, hearts beat fast with anticipation, hands were full of ready gifts. There were the tremulously expectant words of the church service, the night was past and the morning was come, the gifts were given and received, joy and peace made a flapping of wings in each heart, there was a great burst of carols, the Peace of the World had dawned, strife had passed away, every hand was linked in hand, every heart was singing.

D. H. LAWRENCE

Eternal Blessed Life

God didn't send His Son to die
for us so that we could improve
our lives, make better choices,
or feel good about ourselves. We,
who had no life beyond a meager
existence on earth with a few years
of struggle and suffering, now have
the kind of life God intended us
to have all along—eternal, blessed
life.

You and No One Else

Your identity is the result of
neither coincidence nor accident.
You are who you are because of
God's loving design. He wanted
you to be *you*, and no one else.

DARLENE SALA

Sing and Rejoice

What a joy it will be to live with God directly beside us. We look forward to a day when He will walk among His believers (Leviticus 26:12). Though Jesus spent a few years on earth, that wasn't the only time God wanted to spend time with His people. In eternity, He will be right nearby us.

Large Enough

We sometimes fear to bring our
troubles to God, because they
must seem small to Him who
sitteth on the circle of the earth.
But if they are large enough to vex
and endanger our welfare, they are
large enough to touch His heart of
love.

R. A. TORREY

In the Beginning

In the beginning was the Word,
and the Word was with God,
and the Word was God. . . . And
the Word became flesh, and dwelt
among us, and we saw His glory,
glory as of the only begotten from
the Father, full of grace and truth.

JOHN 1:1, 14 NASB

Scripture Index

Old Testament

New Testament